Dear Gameplayer

You are on the explorer ship *Crystal Searcher*.
Your three friends – Jade, Flame and Sky – have gone
to look for the sunken Crystal City on their sub-bike the *Shark*.
But the *Shark* has hit a rock, knocking off its three
propellers and scattering your friends in the depths!

You have three tasks: find and rescue Jade, Flame
and Sky before their air-tanks run out, then find the *Shark*,
repair it by first finding all three of its propellers
(one green, one red and one blue – like those in the
picture on page three), and then go on to
discover the secret of the Crystal City.

Each time you choose a new way to go
you will be told which page to turn to – but there are
many dangers to overcome and puzzles to solve.
Now, you've got your diving suit on, and your
swimming companion Myrtle the Turtle is waiting
below in the Sea of Menace, so off you go!

Good Luck!

Puzzle Master

First published 1998 by Walker Books Ltd
87 Vauxhall Walk, London SE11 5HJ

This edition published 2008

2 4 6 8 10 9 7 5 3 1

Text © 1998 Patrick Burston

Illustrations © 1998 Piers Sanford

The right of Patrick Burston and Piers Sanford to be
identified as author and illustrator respectively of this work
has been asserted by them in accordance with the
Copyright, Designs and Patents Act 1988

This book has been typeset in Galliard

Printed in China

British Library Cataloguing in Publication Data
A catalogue record for this book
is available from the British Library.

ISBN 978-1-4063-1777-0

www.walkerbooks.co.uk

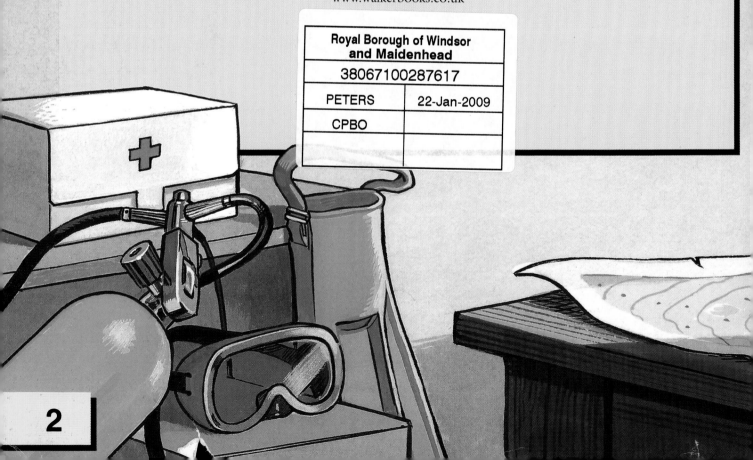

2

PUZZLE MASTER →

The Sea of Menace

Patrick Burston *illustrated by* **Piers Sanford**

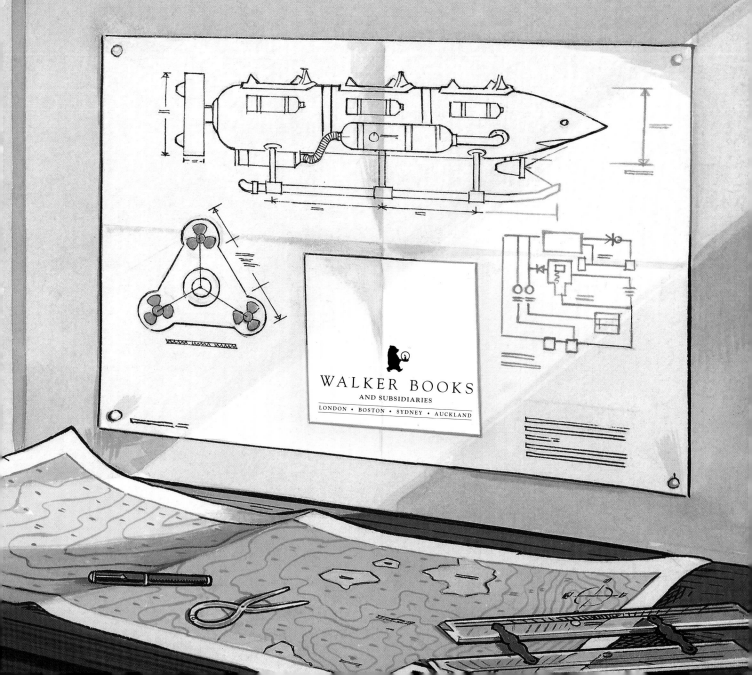

WALKER BOOKS
AND SUBSIDIARIES
LONDON • BOSTON • SYDNEY • AUCKLAND

As you plunge into the depths, three shoals of different coloured fish dart away from you, showing you three different routes you can take. Whichever shoal you choose, there's a fish that doesn't belong. Can you spot it?

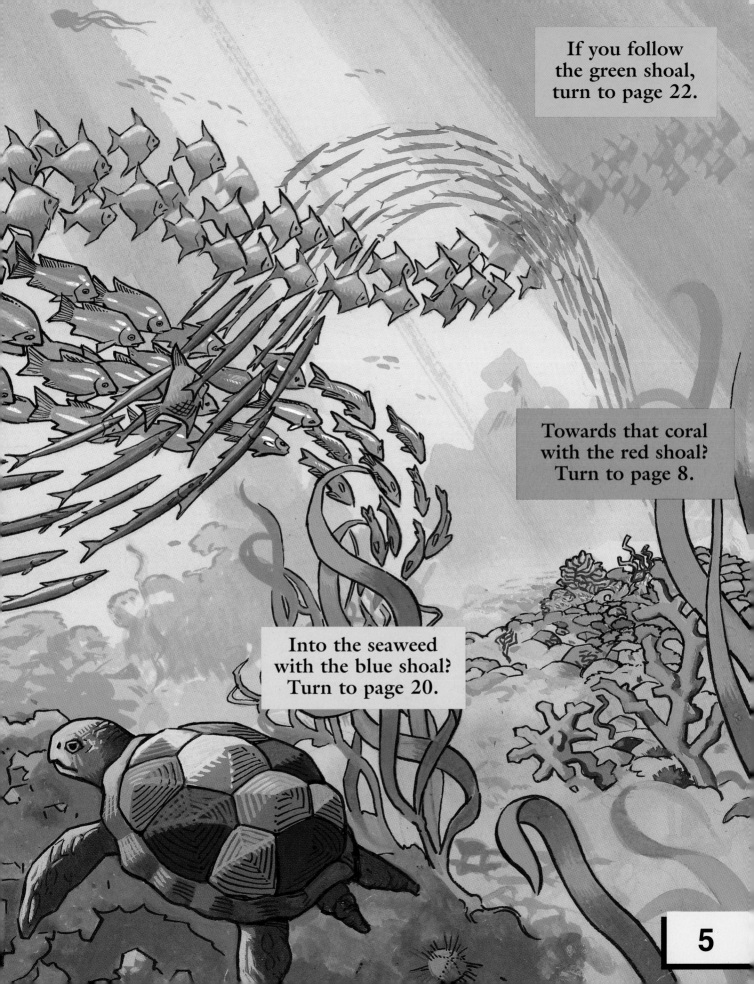

If you follow the green shoal, turn to page 22.

Towards that coral with the red shoal? Turn to page 8.

Into the seaweed with the blue shoal? Turn to page 20.

A sunken wreck … and, among its spilled cargo, Myrtle's found a dangerous package of toxic waste. Find two more packages. Make all three "safe" by finding the outer container that matches the shape of each package.

Old tales say the wreck's haunted, but you'll have to see if one of your friends is inside.

Into the hole in the hull?
Turn to page 34.

Through this door
to page 32.

To page 12.

You've chosen to follow the red-fish route. Look out for the missing red propeller on your journey, but first you must get past this Razor Reef. There are three tunnels through but they're lined with jagged, cutting coral. To protect your hands, find a pair of shells that look like gloves.

To page 14.

To page 38.

You'll have to push your way through this galaxy of starfish! Close your eyes and touch the page with one finger.

If you touch a poisonous purple starfish go back to page 2 for first aid, then start again.

If you touch an orange starfish, go to page 36.

Two twisting whirlpool currents! You could be hurt if you were sucked in at full speed, so pick something parachute-like to slow you down (be careful you don't grab a stinging jellyfish by mistake). Then dive down one of the whirlpools and go where it takes you.

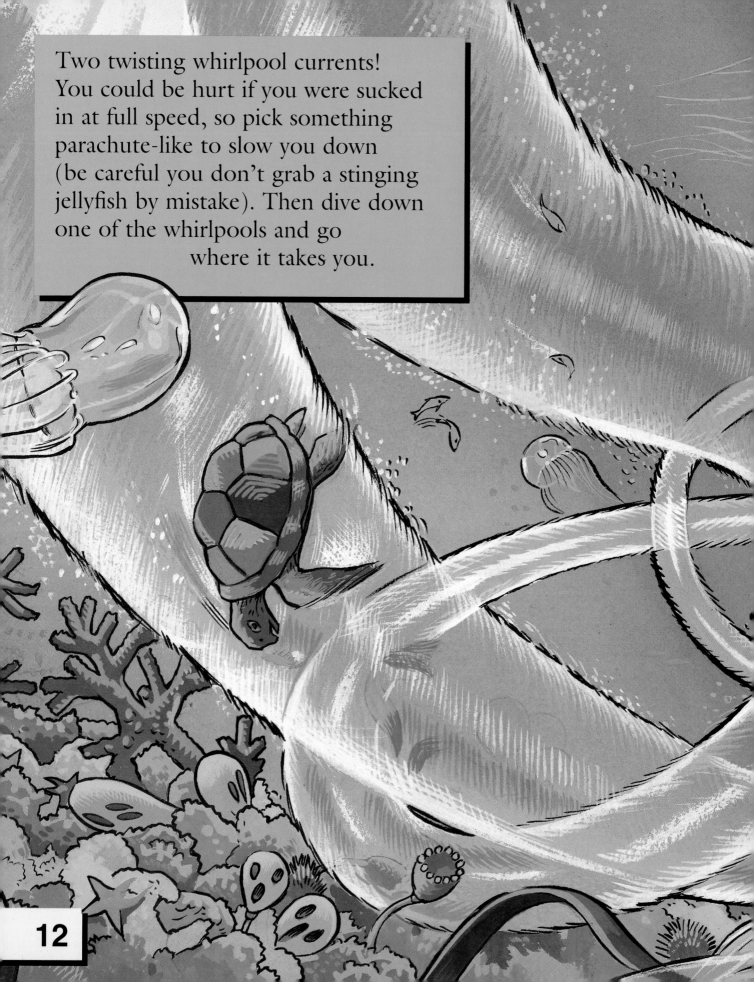

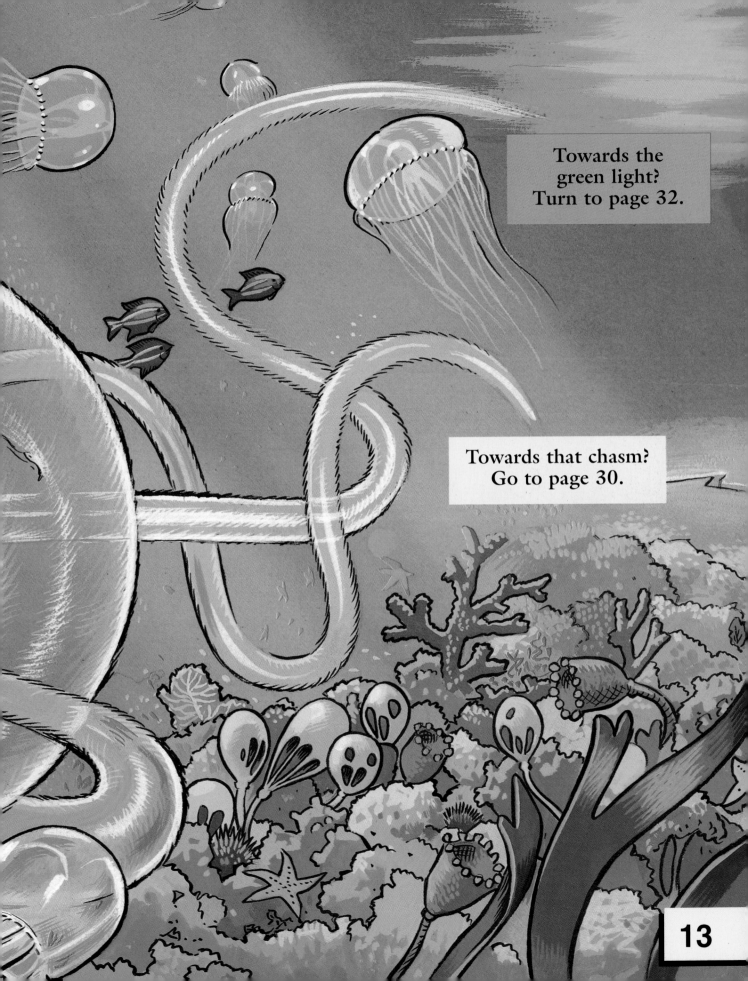

Towards the
green light?
Turn to page 32.

Towards that chasm?
Go to page 30.

13

A huge sponge blocks the cave. Maybe you could wriggle through those big holes in the sponge, but beware, not all the holes reach the other side. If two holes are shaped the same it means you'll go in *and* come out on *this* side! So choose a shape like no other and you'll go right through. And watch out for those grabba-grubs!

14

If you find a single
shape coloured green,
it leads to page 42.

If you find a single
shape coloured pink,
it goes to page 24.

You've found Flame, who's been captured by a giant eel! Find its six babies and it will let Flame go.

Trace or copy the
piece of crystal-disc
Flame's holding – you'll
need it later. Then take
your rescued friend
to page 26.

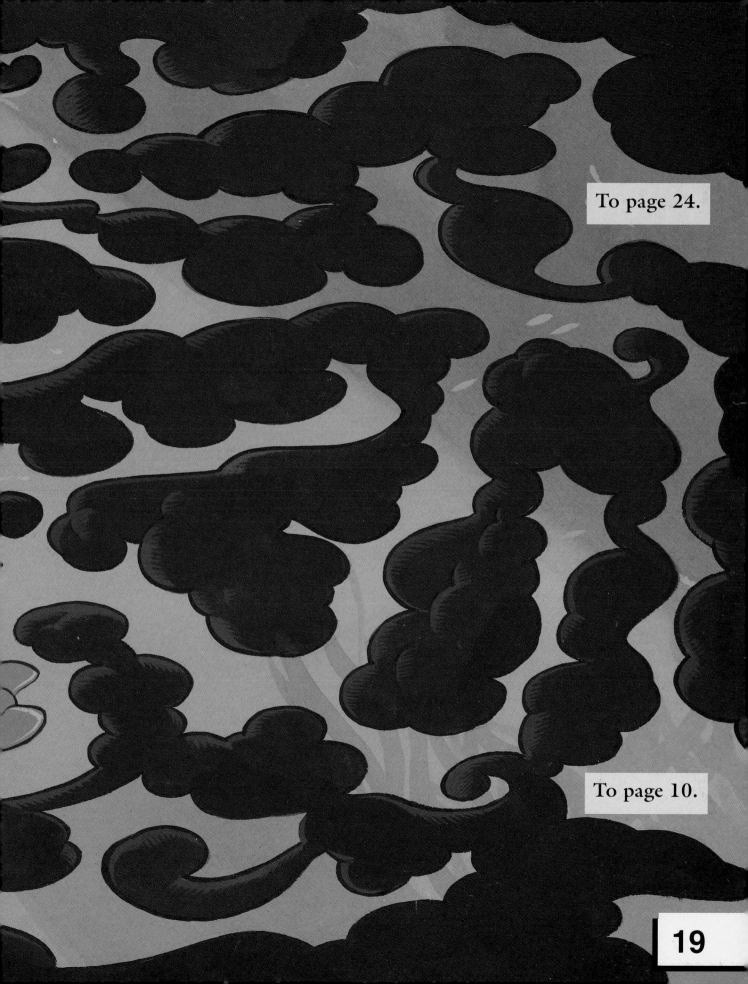

To page 24.

To page 10.

You've chosen the blue-fish route. Look out for the lost blue propeller on your journey, but right now Myrtle's caught in a slimy tangle of tough seaweed. It's not so tough near the base, so find which strand is holding Myrtle, then find something that would cut it!

Towards the inky darkness?
Go to page 18.

The cave leads
to page 14.

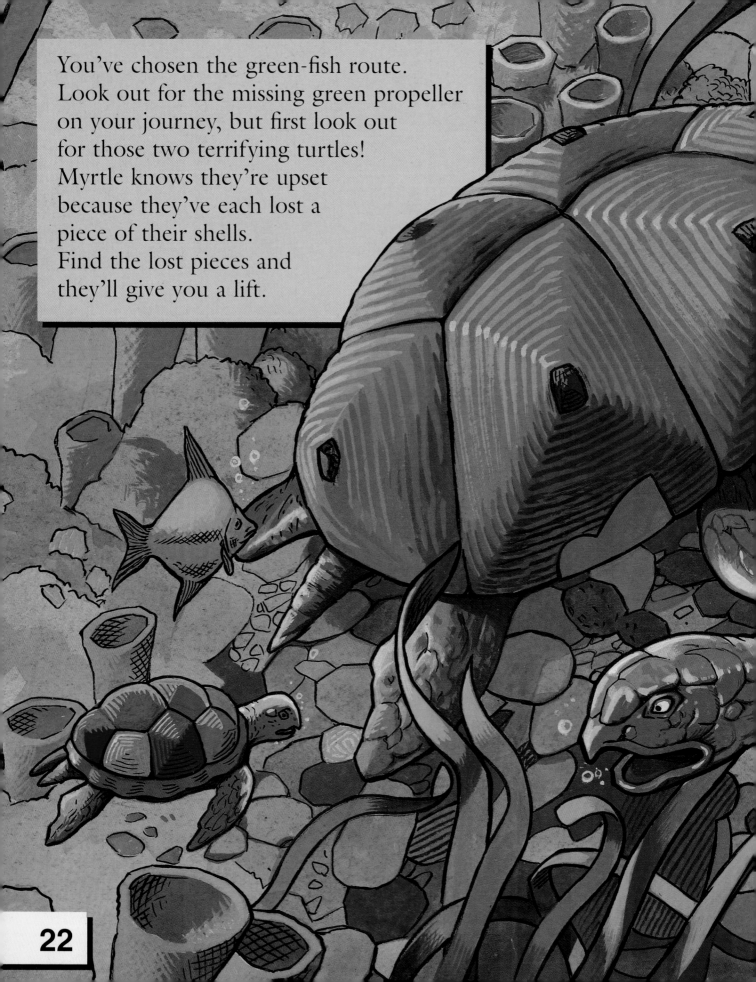

You've chosen the green-fish route.
Look out for the missing green propeller
on your journey, but first look out
for those two terrifying turtles!
Myrtle knows they're upset
because they've each lost a
piece of their shells.
Find the lost pieces and
they'll give you a lift.

Now choose which turtle to ride on.
Count the spots on its shell to find
which page it will take you to.

One touch from these shocktopuses would kill you – and their gravity rays make you too heavy to swim over them! Follow Myrtle and find a way between their terrifying tentacles. (Trace a path with your finger.)

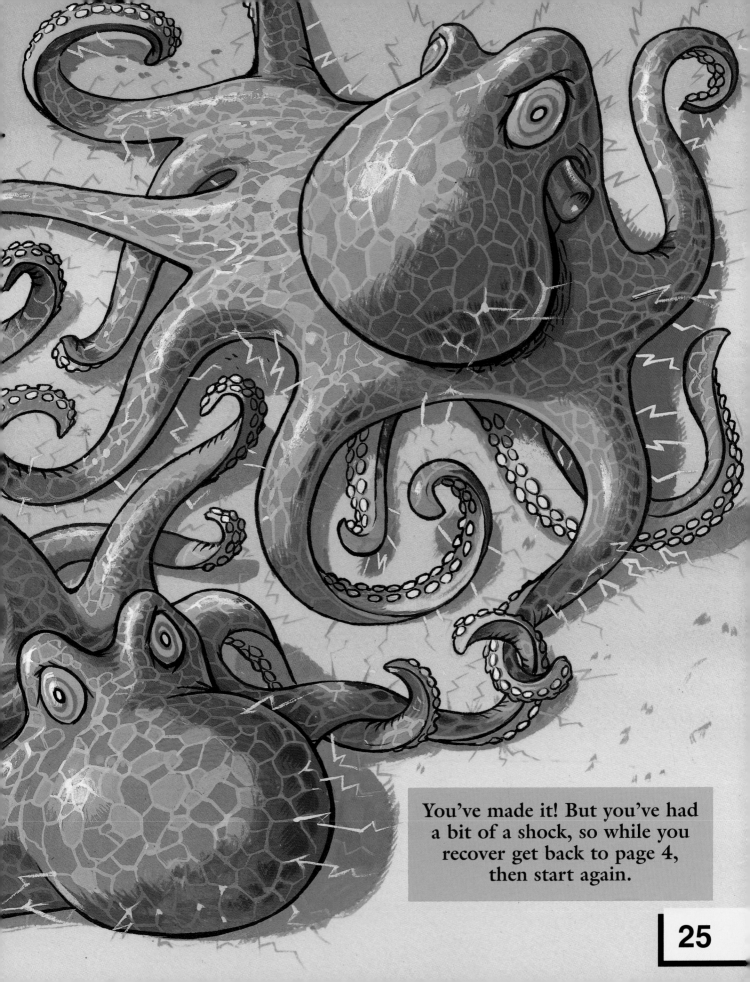

You've made it! But you've had a bit of a shock, so while you recover get back to page 4, then start again.

25

At last, you've found the sub-bike the *Shark*. Now the friend you've just rescued can get a new air-tank and wait here while you rescue another friend (start again from page 4).

Only when you've found all three friends and all three propellers, may you and your friends go on to discover the Crystal City. The mystery page number you need will be revealed when you put the crystal-disc pieces together correctly.

A prehistoric plesiosaur wants to eat Myrtle! First, spot where she's hiding, then find one of those strangely marked stones which matches Myrtle's shell. You can use it to fool the plesiosaur while you both escape.

If you swim this way, go to page 16.

This escape route leads to page 24.

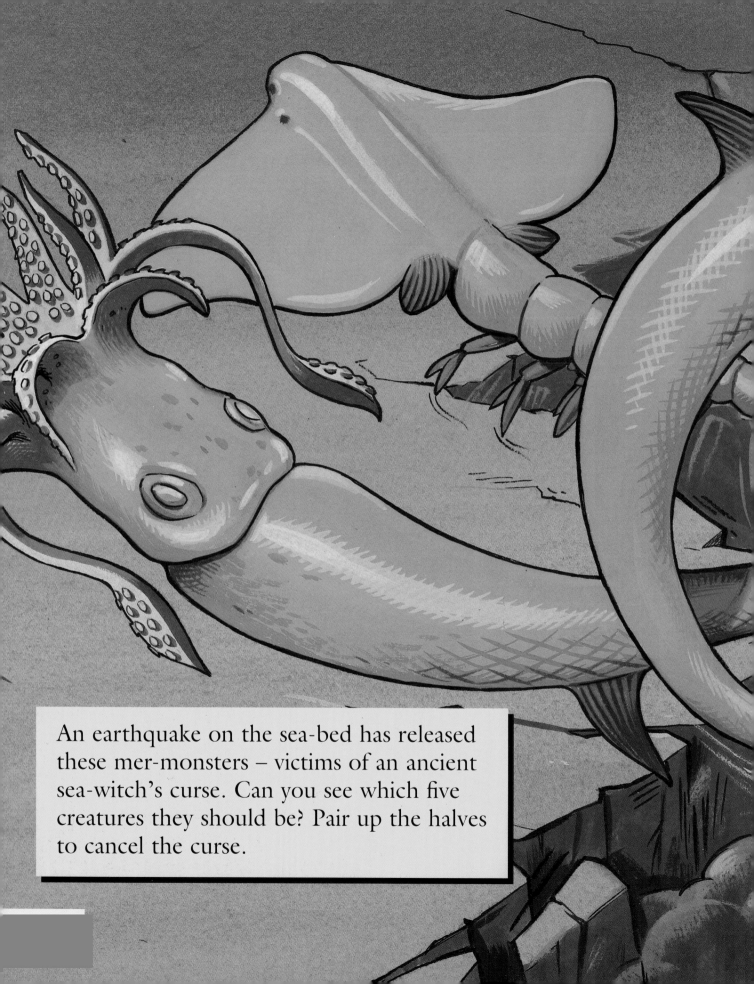

An earthquake on the sea-bed has released these mer-monsters – victims of an ancient sea-witch's curse. Can you see which five creatures they should be? Pair up the halves to cancel the curse.

Better get away from
here before the quake strikes
again! But you still haven't
found all your friends,
so start again from page 4.

31

An upside-down cabin, where the captain was sitting when the ship went down … and he's still sitting in the cabin, haunting it by making eight impossible things happen. Can you find them?

There's only one
way out ... back to
page 4 to start
your quest again!

There's something weird inside the haunted wreck. You can see almost the same view from two portholes. Almost, but not quite. That ghostly pointing hand must have something to do with it!

If you can find ten differences, go through the left-hand porthole to page 40.

If you can't find all ten differences go through the right-hand porthole back to page 4.

Your lost friend Sky has been attacked by a troglobite. It's pulled Sky's helmet off, mistaking it for a blue bloon-pod (the troglobite's favourite food). Hurry, find the missing helmet before Sky drowns … and find five blue bloon-pods to distract the troglobite.

Trace or copy the piece of crystal-disc Sky's holding – you'll need it later. Now take your rescued friend to page 26.

Now take your rescued friend to page 26.

This massive sea anemone has got something you want … can you see what it is and how to get it? Look for something to hook it from the anemone's grasp, then choose which way to go next.

Where's this black cloud coming from? Find out on page 42.

If you go towards those strange stones, go to page 28.

Towards the crack in the sea-bed? Turn to page 30.

Your friend Jade's caught in an old net. You can untie the net if you pull one of those ropes that Myrtle's found. But which is the right rope?

Trace or copy the piece of crystal-disc Jade's holding – you'll need it later. Next, take your rescued friend to page 26.

Well done!
You've stopped
the oil spill –
but to rescue all
your friends
return to
page 4 and
start again.

The Crystal City! Its secret is in those sea-purifying crystal rods growing on top of the crystal dome. One's snapped off and another's grown to replace it. Could you get the broken one and help clean the world's oceans?

Don't swim – the disturbance would shatter the crystal. Start where Myrtle is showing you and climb from one colour to the next in this order: green, red, blue; green, red, blue, and so on.

44

Your tasks are completed – time for you all to return to the *Crystal Searcher* and celebrate!

ANSWERS

6 Green propeller is in large round drum.

12 There is a yellowy-green parachute-plant on the sea-bed.

18 Blue propeller is in ink-maze.

20 Crab pincer on sea-bed.

22 Shell pieces are hidden between pink funnels on right, and below chin of nearest turtle.

28 Myrtle is hiding among stones on left.

30 Squid, swordfish, sea-horse, stingray, lobster.

32
- Ceiling light still on
- Elephant's trunk
- Butterfly
- Impossible porthole view
- Rug should have fallen
- Captain still alive in reflection
- Captain's pipe still smoking
- Books on shelf should have fallen off

38 Hook the red propeller with the anchor chain.

42 The octopus is holding the correct tap.